325.73 Ill
Illegal immigration

$17.45

ЕХАМINI
POLITIC

# Illegal Immigration

## Edited by William Dudley

Daniel Leone, *President*
Bonnie Szumski, *Publisher*
Scott Barbour, *Managing Editor*

**GREENHAVEN
PRESS®**

**THOMSON**
━━━✳━━━ ™
**GALE**

San Diego • Detroit • New York • San Francisco • Cleveland
New Haven, Conn. • Waterville, Maine • London • Munich

© 2003 by Greenhaven Press. Greenhaven Press is an imprint of The Gale Group, Inc., a division of Thomson Learning, Inc.

Greenhaven® and Thomson Learning™ are trademarks used herein under license.

*For more information, contact*
Greenhaven Press
27500 Drake Rd.
Farmington Hills, MI 48331-3535
Or you can visit our Internet site at http://www.gale.com

**ALL RIGHTS RESERVED.**
No part of this work covered by the copyright hereon may be reproduced or used in any form or by any means—graphic, electronic, or mechanical, including photocopying, recording, taping, Web distribution or information storage retrieval systems—without the written permission of the publisher.

Every effort has been made to trace the owners of copyrighted material.

Cover credit: Kelley. © 1994 by Steve Kelley. Reprinted with permission.

**LIBRARY OF CONGRESS CATALOGING-IN-PUBLICATION DATA**

Illegal immigration / William Dudley, book editor.
    p. cm. — (Examining issues through political cartoons)
Includes bibliographical references and index.
ISBN 0-7377-1586-3 (pbk. : alk. paper) — ISBN 0-7377-1585-5 (lib. : alk. paper)
    1. United States—Emigration and immigration—Government policy—Caricatures and cartoons. 2. United States—Emigration and immigration —Caricatures and cartoons. 3. Immigrants—United States—Caricatures and cartoons. I. Dudley, William, 1964–  . II. Series.

JV6483 .I544 2003
325.73'022'2—dc21

2002040815

Printed in the United States of America

# Contents

# Foreword

Political cartoons, also called editorial cartoons, are drawings that do what editorials do with words—express an opinion about a newsworthy event or person. They typically appear in the opinion pages of newspapers, sometimes in support of that day's written editorial, but more often making their own comment on the day's events. Political cartoons first gained widespread popularity in Great Britain and the United States in the 1800s when engravings and other drawings skewering political figures were fashionable in illustrated newspapers and comic magazines. By the beginning of the 1900s, editorial cartoons were an established feature of daily newspapers. Today, they can be found throughout the globe in newspapers, magazines, and online publications and the Internet.

Art Wood, both a cartoonist and a collector of cartoons, writes in his book *Great Cartoonists and Their Art:*

> Day in and day out the cartoonist mirrors history; he reduces complex facts into understandable and artistic terminology. He is a political commentator and at the same time an artist.

The distillation of ideas into images is what makes political cartoons a valuable resource for studying social and historical topics. Editorial cartoons have a point to express. Analyzing them involves determining both what the cartoon's point is and how it was made.

Sometimes, the point made by the cartoon may be one that the reader disagrees with, or considers offensive. Such cartoons expose readers to new ideas and thereby challenge them to analyze and question their own opinions and assumptions. In some extreme cases, cartoons provide vivid examples of the thoughts that lie behind heinous

4

acts; for example, the cartoons created by the Nazis illustrate the anti-Semitism that led to the mass persecution of Jews.

Examining controversial ideas is but one way the study of political cartoons can enhance and develop critical thinking skills. Another aspect to cartoons is that they can use symbols to make their point quickly. For example, in a cartoon in *Euthanasia*, Chuck Asay depicts supporters of a legal "right to die" by assisted suicide as vultures. Vultures are birds that eat dead and dying animals and are often a symbol of repulsive and cowardly predators who take advantage of those who have met misfortune or are vulnerable. The reader can infer that Asay is expressing his opposition to physician-assisted suicide by suggesting that its supporters are just as loathsome as vultures. Asay thus makes his point through a quick symbolic association.

An important part of critical thinking is examining ideas and arguments in their historical context. Political cartoonists (reasonably) assume that the typical reader of a newspaper's editorial page already has a basic knowledge of current issues and newsworthy people. Understanding and appreciating political cartoons often requires such knowledge, as well as a familiarity with common icons and symbolic figures (such as Uncle Sam's representing the United States). The need for contextual information becomes especially apparent in historical cartoons. For example, although most people know who Adolf Hitler is, a lack of familiarity with other German political figures of the 1930s may create difficulty in fully understanding cartoons about Nazi Germany made in that era.

Providing such contextual information is one important way that Greenhaven's Examining Issues Through Political Cartoons series seeks to make this unique and revealing resource conveniently accessible to students. Each volume presents a representative and diverse collection of political cartoons focusing on a particular current or historical topic. An introductory essay provides a general overview of the subject matter. Each cartoon is then presented with accompanying information including facts about the cartoonist and information and commentary on the cartoon itself. Finally, each volume contains additional informational resources, including listings of books, articles, and websites; an index; and (for historical topics) a chronology of events. Taken together, the contents of each anthology constitute an amusing and informative resource for students of historical and social topics.

5

# Introduction

The Statue of Liberty, a gift from the French government to America, was designed to be a monument to liberty and republicanism. However, soon after its erection in New York City in 1886, it became something else—a symbol of America's welcoming attitude toward immigrants entering the country. For many of the estimated 12 million immigrants (mostly from Europe) who passed through the government reception center at Ellis Island between 1892 and 1932, the statue was the first American sight they witnessed. A poem by Emma Lazarus, inscribed at the statue's base, made the connection between the statue and immigration clear:

> Give me your tired, your poor,
> Your huddled masses yearning to breathe free,
> The wretched refuse of your teeming shore.
> Send these, the homeless, tempest-tossed to me:
> I lift my lamp beside the golden door.

The statue's connection in the public mind with immigration contains several ironies, beyond the fact that the monument was not originally meant to symbolize America's embrace of immigrants. One is what historian Roger Daniels has called the "Statue of Liberty myth" that all immigrants were dirt poor. Daniels and other historians have argued that careful study reveals that American immigrants, instead of "wretched refuse," tended to be better off and better educated than the average resident of their country of origin. Another irony is the fact that, contrary to the poem's theme of welcoming immigrants, the United States has long had restrictions on immigration. An 1882 federal law excluded Chinese from immigrating to the United States. Other federal laws forbade immigrants with criminal records or radical political opinions. In the early 1900s informal agreements between the Japanese and American governments restricted Japanese immigration. A 1917 federal law instituted a literacy test for immigrants. In 1921 and 1924, federal immigration laws against immigration were expanded to bar virtually all Asians and to establish national quotas that limited immigration from many European countries. Also in 1924, the United States Border Patrol—a new government agency with the power to arrest and deport illegal immigrants—was created to curtail illegal immigrant crossings from Mexico and Canada.

While immigration laws have been liberalized since then, eliminating the national origins quota system, the Border Patrol still operates and America still has a policy of restricting immigration. Foreigners often wait years to obtain one of the seven hundred thousand immigrant visas the American government issues annually. Because demand for such visas exceeds supply, many people decide to forgo the legal process and simply enter the United States without permission. Some slip into the country without a visa. Others enter on temporary, nonimmigrant visas (such as tourist visas or student visas), but then stay after their visas expire. Others enter with fraudulent documents. Estimates on the size of the illegal immigration population in the United States vary from 2 to 11 million. The Immigration and Naturalization Service (INS), the federal bureaucracy charged with enforcing immigration laws, estimated in a 1997 report that 5 million illegal immigrants resided in the United States in 1996. The Census Bureau in 2000 estimated the population of illegal residents to be 8.5 million, up from 3.5 million in 1990.

Illegal immigrants have been a divisive element throughout American history. For all the Statue of Liberty–inspired rhetoric about America's being an immigrant nation, Americans have often had an uneasy and ambivalent relationship with new immigrants. "We view immigrants with rose-colored glasses, turned backward," argues scholar Rita Simon. The celebration of America's immigrant history can obscure the divisive and negative reactions many immigrants created when they first arrived. Throughout the nation's history, many Americans have viewed immigrants with alarm and held that their continuing influx threatened America. Arguments made for and against immigrants have remained remarkably constant over time.

# Welfare Concerns

A common past and present complaint about immigrants, both legal and illegal, is that they are so poor and unskilled as to be unable to support themselves, and thus are at risk of becoming an economic burden. A report made in 1819 by the Society for the Prevention of Pauperism in New York argued that growing numbers of European immigrants were creating a serious problem. Europe, they argued had

> an almost innumerable population . . . [that] is out of employment. . . . This country is the resort of vast numbers of these needy and wretched beings. . . . They are frequently found destitute in our streets: they seek employment at our doors: they are found in our almshouses and in our hospitals.

These complaints were echoed thirty years later by Kentucky senator Garrett Davis, who argued in a 1849 speech that England and other European nations "have put into operation extensive and well-arranged systems of emigrating and transporting to America their excess of population, and particularly the refuse, the pauper, the demoralized, and the criminal." They were repeated by sociologist Edward A. Ross, who in a 1914 book decried Italian immigrants who

> apply for once for relief with their air, "Here we are. Now what are you going to do for us?" They even *insist* on relief as a right. At home it had been noised about that in foolish America baskets of food are actually sent in to the needy, and some are coming over expressly to obtain such largesse.

In response to such criticism, federal immigration laws as early as 1882 sought to screen out "paupers" and make would-be immigrants prove they have a means of support so they would not become government charges. Legal immigrants today are barred from most federal welfare programs. One result of this evolution of immigration laws is that welfare-related arguments against immigrants now focus on illegal immigrants. A fairly recent example of such criticism can be found in the campaign in California over Proposition 187, an initiative that appeared on the state ballot in 1994. Proposition 187 proposed denying public education, health, and social service benefits to illegal immigrants. Its supporters argued that California was spending billions of dollars on social welfare for illegal immigrants. George Sunderland, arguing for Proposition 187, claimed that "droves of illegals routinely enter California in order to obtain that state's high level of welfare payments." California voters passed the proposition, but most of its provisions were overturned by federal courts.

Defenders of immigrants, both past and present, have questioned whether illegal immigrants are as costly as their critics make them out to be. "I have found nothing to prove that the foreign born contribute more largely to the almshouse population . . . than do the native whites of the same sex and age residing in the *same* part of the country," *Independent* magazine contributor W.F. Willcox wrote in 1912. Seventy-five years later, civil rights activists Raúl Hinojosa and Peter Schey, arguing against Proposition 187, noted that illegal immigrants pay significant amounts in federal, state, and local taxes. Furthermore, they argue,

> undocumented immigrants actually use social services far less than the typical working-class household. This is not surprising given that federal law already renders undocumented immigrants ineligible for most social and health services. Moreover, recent immigrants tend to be healthier than the typical U.S. citizen.

Illegal immigrants are an economic asset, not a burden, in this view.

## Labor Concerns

Defenders of immigrants often responded to the charge that immigrants consume welfare resources by arguing that immigrants do not come to America to seek charity or welfare, but to better their condition through work. However, the role of immigrant labor has itself been a central factor of Americans' ambivalence toward its immigrants. Many labor organizations have long advocated stricter immigration limits and stronger enforcement of existing rules, arguing that the willingness of immigrants to work for low wages undercuts the standard of living for other Americans. By competing for work with American workers and accepting lower wages, immigrants displace American workers and drive down average wages of working-class people. "When an immigrant without resources is compelled to accept work at less than the established wage rate," argued American Federation of Labor president John Mitchell in 1914, "he not only displaces a man working at the higher rate, but his action threatens to destroy the whole schedule of wages in the industry in which he secures employment." Legislation passed within a decade of Mitchell's complaint fulfilled some of his goals of restricting immigration and wage competition from immigrants. However, illegal immigrants have continued to enter the country. Their willingness to work for low wages stems in part, critics claim, from fear of being caught and deported if they organized unions or sought higher pay. In 1999, the Federation for American Immigration Reform, in an argument nearly identical to Mitchell's, contended that

> immigration harms the American workforce . . . [because of] displacement, that is, when established workers, whether natives or immigrants, lose their jobs to new immigrants, often illegal newcomers, who will work for substandard wages. . . . Firms that use immigrants—and pay them low wages—underbid the firms that use natives.

Past and present supporters of immigration have countered that immigrants were not "taking" jobs from Americans because they performed tasks that Americans did not want to do. "Our American workers look with more or less disdain upon the handling of the pick and shovel," argued merchant and philanthropist Harris Weinstock in 1916. "Whatever the causes may be, they do not and will not perform the unavoidable tasks inseparable from the development of great natural resources." Another need immigrants fill, he argues, is housework. "For social and other reasons American girls will not, as a rule, enter domestic service," he asserted in his 1916 article. The shortage of such help "is a menace to the American home."

Today much of this work—both unskilled labor and domestic service—is performed by illegal immigrants, and similar arguments can be found praising them for it. Author Tamar Jacoby, writing in the *Wall Street Journal* in 2002, asserted that

> it's no accident that 80% of our farm workers are foreign-born. Americans simply won't do menial work at prevailing wages. The immigrants who increasingly fill the dirtiest and most dangerous industrial jobs keep these jobs here—

without them, the work would migrate to countries where labor is cheaper. And their purchases sustain all other manner of American businesses.

However, Michael Scott, a California businessman, contends that it is "the biggest lie of all" that "Americans won't do the work that illegals perform." He argues that "the truth is that . . . Americans won't live in garages with multiple families . . . or . . . take on backbreaking work at below minimum wages. Get rid of illegal immigrants and wages would have to rise."

Such clashing views on illegal immigration and work can be seen in the case of Tyson Foods, a large corporation that was indicted in December 2001 for allegedly running an illegal immigrant smuggling and hiring ring. Critics of the corporation accused it of recruiting illegal immigrants because they would accept below-market wages and working conditions that U.S. citizens would reject. A *Dallas Morning News* editorial argued that greedy employers seek illegal immigrants because "they work hard for low wages and rarely complain or unionize especially if undocumented. For employers who put profit first, the temptation to exploit that combination can be irresistible." But columnist Charles Oliver responds that "those who understand how markets work may not be so quick to condemn Tyson. . . . The company desperately needed workers for jobs that most Americans won't take. Someone has to do the dirty work of transforming a live bird into a boneless, skinless chicken breast."

Employing illegal immigrants was itself made into a crime in the 1986 Immigration Reform and Control Act (IRCA). In 1996 President Bill Clinton issued an executive order prohibiting companies that knowingly hire illegal immigrants from competing for federal contracts. But immigration critics argue that enforcement of such laws has been spotty.

## Crime and Security Concerns

In addition to labor and welfare, arguments against immigrants have drawn on public safety concerns. Some arguments focus on an alleged higher propensity for crime among the immigrant population. In the early 1900s, many people viewed with alarm the large wave of immigrants from southern and eastern Europe. "I don't want to say anything that would be indiscreet," stated New York City's police commissioner (cited in a 1910 report by the Immigration Restriction League),

> but unquestionably the hordes of immigrants that are coming here have a good deal to do with crimes against women and children. . . . It is this wave of immigration that brings to New York the hundreds of thousands of criminals who don't know what liberty means, and don't care; don't know our customs . . . and are in general the scum of Europe.

Similar arguments are often heard against illegal immigrants today, often bolstered by the notion that because illegal immigrants are breaking the law by simply being here, they may therefore be more likely as a group to break other laws. "This disrespect for the law," argues columnist Josh Moenning, "leads to . . . crimes that illegal aliens often commit while they reside here. Overcrowded prisons are often a complaint in areas with a high level of illegal immigration. In addition, narcotics often find their way to this country across the border, smuggled in by aliens." Concerns such as those voiced by Moenning were in part responsible for passage of the 1996 Illegal Immigration Reform and Responsibility Act (IIRRA), which mandated that the INS detain and deport any noncitizen who had been convicted of certain crimes.

Defenders of immigrants, past and present, have responded by arguing that immigrants are no more likely to commit crimes than any other group. "Taken as a whole," argued Peter Roberts in a 1912 book examining the "new" immigrants from southern and eastern Europe,

> they do not show moral turpitude above the average of civilized men. Although transplanted into a new environment, living under abnormal conditions in industrial centers, and meeting more temptation in a week than they would in a lifetime in rural communities in the homeland, yet when their criminal record is compared with that of the native-born males, it comes out better than even.

Identical arguments can be found in the present day. Anne Carr, an attorney, asserted in a 1999 article that "immigrants do not commit proportionately more crimes than American citizens do," a fact "true of both legal and illegal immigrants." Carr made this claim in an article highly critical of the IIRRA, which she contends removes all flexibility and discretion from America's immigration system, and could be applied retroactively for minor crimes. "A legal resident with a second shoplifting offense from 1975 is now likely to be classified as an aggravated felon and find herself on the plane home with no possibility of forgiveness."

In addition to being linked with individual and organized crime, immigrants have often been charged with acting on behalf of America's enemies or of "infecting" America with dangerous foreign ideologies or belief systems. The specific foreign ideology has changed as America's perceived enemies have changed. In the mid–nineteenth century, when millions of German and Irish Catholics were immigrating to the United States, Roman Catholicism was perceived as a serious foreign threat to the American way of life. Samuel F.B. Morse, the inventor of the telegraph, argued in an 1835 article that European governments were deliberately attempting to flood America with Catholic immigrants, selecting them "not for the affinity to liberty, but for their mental servitude and their docility in obeying the orders of their priests." But as Catholic immigrants assimilated and became more accepted in America, Catholicism faded as a threat.

The 1917 Bolshevik Revolution in Russia, coupled with labor unrest in America after World War I, made radicals and Communists a leading threat in the minds of many Americans. A series of bomb scares in 1919 heightened public fears. In 1920 Attorney General A. Mitchell Palmer led a nationwide mass arrest of six thousand suspected anarchists and radicals—most of them immigrants from Russia and eastern Europe—and held them captive for weeks without charges being brought against them. Palmer explained his reasons for his actions in a 1920 magazine article:

> My information showed that communism in this country was an organization of thousands of aliens. . . . It showed they were making the same glittering promises of lawlessness, of criminal autocracy to Americans, that they had made to Russian peasants. . . . The Government is now sweeping the nation clean of such alien filth. . . . It is my belief that while they have stirred discontent in our midst,

while they have caused irritating strikes, and while they have infected our social ideas with the disease of their own minds and their unclean morals, we can get rid of them!

The "Palmer Raids" resulted in the deportation of 556 aliens and the confiscation of three handguns. Most of the prisoners were eventually released. But while that particular "red scare" abated after 1921, fear of bolshevism and other radical ideas supposedly harbored by foreign immigrants was part of the reason Congress passed restrictive immigration laws in the 1920s.

History repeated itself in the early twenty-first century, only this time the foreign threat was Islamic-sponsored terrorism. The September 11, 2001, terrorist attacks that were carried out by nineteen foreign residents in America from Saudi Arabia and other Arab nations was the largest of several disturbing incidents. In 1993 a Pakistani immigrant was charged with ambushing and shooting several employees of the Central Intelligence Agency. The following year, four Islamic terrorists were convicted of bombing the World Trade Center in New York City. Much as fear of radicalism was directed at eastern European immigrants in the 1920s, fear of terrorism was directed at American residents from Arab and Muslim nations. "We have . . . the scenario of millions, just millions of illegal aliens in our midst," asserted George Gekas, a member of Congress and chair of the House Immigration Subcommittee, in June 2002. "There are thousands among those millions, perhaps millions among those millions, who have exactly that kind of mindset to do harm to our country, to be or become terrorists."

Since the September 11, 2001, terrorist attacks, the U.S. government has detained more than twelve hundred immigrants residing in the United States, most of them from Muslim nations. Hundreds of these aliens were held in solitary confinement in secret locations for months; around five hundred were then deported for immigration violations. Attorney General John Ashcroft has defended these actions as a necessary part of the war on terrorism. In an August 7, 2002, speech, he stated that "our most important objective is to save innocent lives from further acts of terrorism by identifying, disrupting, and dismantling terrorist networks" and that every person arrested had been "detained under the law." But Deborah Jacobs, executive director of the Newark chapter of the American Civil

Liberties Union, has argued that "we are selectively enforcing our immigration laws, and there is a vengeance to it." Anthony Romero, national executive director of the ACLU, argues that certain foreign immigrants are being unfairly singled out. "Pakistanis, Muslims, Arabs, and others . . . [faced] greater scrutiny because of their national origin and religion."

## The Role of Racism and Prejudice

A glaring exception to the tendency of past anti-immigrant arguments to be similar to present-day ones is in the area of race. The literature on immigrants in the nineteenth and early twentieth centuries is full of very explicit and open references to superior and inferior races. A common argument among anti-immigrant activists was that through unlimited immigration, America was letting inferior peoples in and endangering its future. Such appeals to race prejudice are difficult to find in immigrant arguments today.

The targets of racial arguments against immigrants have changed as American immigration patterns changed. One historical example of racism was the anti-Asian movement of the 1870s that was responding to the influx of Chinese workers and immigrants to California and other western states; it culminated in the passage of the Chinese Exclusion Act of 1882. Proponents of Chinese exclusion used various economic and other arguments for restricting Chinese immigration, but racist motives were also clear. California governor Leland Stanford called the Chinese "a degraded and distinct people" who had "deleterious influence upon the superior [white] race." The prejudicial aspects of arguments against Chinese immigrants were noted by Massachusetts senator George F. Hoar, who in arguing against the Chinese Exclusion Act decried "the old race prejudice, very fruitful of crime and of folly," and asserted that similar prejudicial arguments had been raised against Irish immigrants decades before.

With the Chinese and most other Asians effectively excluded from the United States at the beginning of the twentieth century, racial concerns focused on the rising numbers of immigrants from southern and eastern Europe. Prescott F. Hall, one of the founders of the influential Immigration Restriction League created in 1894, argued that the question facing Americans was whether their country was "to be peopled by British, German, and Scandinavian stock, historically free, energetic, progressive, or by Slav, Latin and Asiatic races historically down-trodden, atavistic, and stagnant." Kenneth Roberts, writing in the popular *Saturday Evening Post* in 1923, argued against admitting Polish Jews as immigrants, calling them "human parasites," and claimed that mixing Anglo-Saxons with people from other ethnic groups would result in a "hybrid race of people as worthless and futile as the good-for-nothing mongrels of Central America and Southeastern Europe." Such arguments helped lead to the 1921 and 1924 immigration laws that restricted immigration from suspect parts of the world.

These restrictive laws were reformed in 1965; since then only a small fraction of American immigrants have come from Europe (much less northern Europe). Today's "new" immigrants (both legal and illegal) come mostly from Asia and Latin America. In his 1996 book *Alien Nation*, author Peter Brimelow decries this trend, arguing that "the American nation has always had a specific ethnic core. And that core has been white." Continued illegal and legal immigration, he argued, threatened to "break down white America's sense of identity." But most immigration opponents have carefully avoided arguing in such racial terms. Thanks in part to the civil rights movement of the 1950s and 1960s, open expressions of racial superiority and inferiority are widely discredited. "Nowadays it is no longer acceptable to publicly state crude racist arguments about color, ethnicity and religion," argued economist Julian Simon in a 1990 article. But he goes on to claim that "bigotry remains a driving force behind immigration opposition." Whether or not Simon's accusation is true is itself a matter of debate.

## Views of America

The issue of illegal immigration promises to be a continuing controversy in the twenty-first century, just as it was in the nineteenth and twentieth centuries, in part because it touches on so many other issues including race, the role of government, crime, and social change. Many of the views and arguments expressed in 1882, 1924, or 2001 will probably find similar expression in the future. Perhaps most profoundly, illegal immigration will continue to raise questions of national identity. Does the Statue of Liberty still represent American ideals of welcoming immigrants and refugees from around the world? Are illegal immigrants enemies of America, or part of what makes America special and strong? For some people, immigrants who break the law to come here are fundamentally un-American. For others, these seekers of a better life in this country are the quintessential Americans. "Ultimately, this is a debate about values, not money," asserts writer Richard Rayner, a novelist who himself immigrated to America from England. "This is about how America feels about itself." The cartoons in this volume, some old, some new, provide expressions not only of immigrants and immigration, but express the artists' views on the United States itself.

# Chapter 1

# Historical Views of Immigration

# Preface

Illegal immigration has been a policy issue in the United States as far back as 1882, when Congress passed laws banning the immigration of paupers, convicts, and all immigrants from China. Although Chinese immigrants made up only .002 percent of America's population at the time, many Americans had voiced concerns that Chinese laborers took jobs from Americans and lowered workers' wages. In addition, the Chinese were seen as an alien people who were a threat to America's white "racial purity." The population of Chinese immigrants sharply declined after the 1882 Chinese Exclusion Act was passed, although some Chinese still continued to slip into the country, becoming some of the nation's first illegal immigrants.

Although the Chinese were for many years the only nationality to be excluded by immigration laws, other immigrant groups were also often held in contempt by many Americans during the nineteenth and early twentieth centuries. Nativist (anti-immigrant) sentiment was at first directed mostly against Roman Catholic immigrants from Germany and Ireland. Critics of Catholicism asserted that it was incompatible with America's republican system of government. By the late nineteenth century, fears of radical movements had replaced anti-Catholicism as a driving motivation behind anti-immigrant feeling. At a time when the industrial revolution was transforming the economy and working conditions in the United States, many Americans blamed immigrants for the labor unrest of the period.

Racism and ethnic prejudice also led many Americans to view immigrants as "undesirable." Such prejudice was directed not only against the Irish and Chinese, but also against the millions of immigrants from Italy, Greece, Russia, and other southern and eastern European nations, which replaced northwestern Europe as America's leading source of immigration after 1890. In the 1920s, Congress responded to public fears of foreign "invasion" by passing new laws that sharply limited immigration. The laws included quotas that either banned or severely limited immigration from Asia and southern and eastern Europe.

The sometimes harsh public attitudes toward immigrants in the nineteenth and early twentieth centuries is amply demonstrated in the political cartoons of the time, many of which featured crude stereotypes of Chinese, Irish, and other immigrant groups. However, not all Americans viewed immigrants in a negative light. Immigrants of all types have also been defended and praised for their industriousness, their ability to adapt to American life, and for other contributions to the nation. Critics of immigrants have themselves been criticized for holding on to racist and discredited prejudices. "Is it not high time that we, conceited, self-contained, arrogant Americans should recognize that these strangers that flock to our gates come, many of them, bearing precious gifts?" asked religious leader Charles D. Williams in a 1923 book. The following chapter features some examples of both positive and negative portrayals of immigrants in American history.

# Examining Cartoon 1:
# "The Chinese Question"

**THE CHINESE QUESTION.—**
COLUMBIA.– "HANDS OFF, GENTLEMEN! AMERICA MEANS FAIR PLAY FOR ALL MEN."

# About the Cartoon

The first U.S. law that excluded certain immigrants was the 1882 Chinese Exclusion Act. Public support for such a measure had been building up for some time, especially in the western states where most of the Chinese had settled, but also in places like New York City. Chinese immigrants were condemned as heathens who undercut workers' wages and corrupted American culture with foreign ways; in some places they were physically attacked by mobs. Ironically, many of the most outspoken anti-Chinese activists, such as San Francisco leader Dennis Kearney, were immigrants from Ireland and other countries.

Famed political cartoonist Thomas Nast presents his perspective on Chinese immigration and its opponents in this 1871 cartoon, which first appeared in *Harper's Weekly* magazine. The drawing features "Columbia" —a noble woman who was a symbol of the New World and its ideals—defending a Chinese immigrant from a mob. The mob consists of Irish and German Americans—groups that were frequently the target of Nast's work. The cartoon is partly a defense of American ideals of fairness (the caption reads in part "America means fair play for all men"), partly a sympathetic portrayal of the Chinese immigrant, and partly an attack on German and Irish immigrants. Nast mocks the last group for equating real culture with "white culture" and suggests that they do not have much moral standing to criticize the Chinese. The reference to the "Colored Orphan Asylum" in the background, for instance, is a visual reminder of an ugly incident in 1863, when an orphanage for black children was burned by Irish Americans in a New York City riot.

# About the Cartoonist

Thomas Nast, a German-born immigrant who moved to America as a child, began his career as an illustrator for *Harper's Weekly* and *Frank Leslie's Illustrated Newspaper* and gained nationwide fame for his illustrations of the Civil War. His work for *Harper's Weekly* in the 1860s and 1870s is credited with creating and developing the modern political cartoon. His cartoons of New York City political leader William M. "Boss" Tweed helped bring about the downfall of Tweed and his Tammany Hall political machine.

Nast. © 1871 by *Harper's Weekly*.

# Examining Cartoon 2:
# "Welcome to All"

**WELCOME TO ALL!**

## About the Cartoon

Until the late nineteenth century, American immigration policy remained largely true to President George Washington's assertion that the "bosom of America is open to receive not only the opulent and respected stranger, but the oppressed and persecuted of all nations and religions." This 1880 cartoon celebrates this idea of America as a land of refuge. Inspired by the biblical story of the flood, it features Uncle Sam in the position of Noah welcoming passengers to the ark. Instead of animals fleeing a global flood, the refugees are couples from varying nationalities and backgrounds who are fleeing oppressive governments in Europe. The United States, in contrast to Europe, is a land of freedom. Between 1880 and 1924 some 24 million foreigners came to America, many of them refugees escaping political repression and economic hardship.

## About the Cartoonist

Joseph Keppler was Thomas Nast's chief rival political cartoonist of the era. Like Nast, Keppler was a German-born immigrant and a former illustrator for *Frank Leslie's Illustrated Newspaper*. In 1876 he founded *Puck*, America's first humor magazine (and one of the first to use color illustrations). The cartoons in that weekly "were awaited eagerly, were passed from hand to hand, and were the subject of animated comment in all political circles," according to writer Joseph P. Bishop.

Keppler. © 1870 by *Puck*.

# Examining Cartoon 3:
# "No Dumping Ground For Refuse"

# About the Cartoon

By the 1920s public sentiment in America had turned against immigration. Opponents feared that the newcomers were taking away American jobs and were spreading dangerous new socialist and radical ideas. Racial, ethnic, and religious prejudice—against Asians, dark-skinned Europeans from southern and eastern Europe, Catholics, and Jews—also played a role. This 1921 cartoon by Lute Pease depicts the argument that America was being used as a "dumping ground" for "undesirables" from Europe. In 1924 Congress passed new laws that set strict limits on immigration from both Asia and from southern and eastern Europe.

# About the Cartoonist

Lute Pease, a former gold prospector in Alaska, worked for more than thirty years, beginning in 1914, as the editorial cartoonist for the *Newark Evening News*. He won the Pulitzer Prize for editorial cartoons in 1949, five weeks after his eightieth birthday.

Pease. © 1921 by *Newark Evening News*.

# Chapter 2

# Illegal Immigrants and Immigration Policy

# Preface

Rafael Vega, an Illinois resident featured in a *Chicago Tribune* article, is a hard worker who drives to several factory jobs. He wants to obtain a driver's license, but is unable to because he cannot provide a Social Security number on the application. Vega is an illegal immigrant, one of an estimated three hundred thousand in the state of Illinois.

Vega's dilemma illustrates the types of predicaments illegal immigrants face, but it also reveals a societal divide over how immigrants should be treated. Some states, such as North Carolina and Utah, have made illegal immigrants eligible for driver's licenses. Proponents of this policy argue that it makes the roads safer for everyone by ensuring that all drivers pass tests and have insurance. Opponents counter that such a policy enables illegal immigrants to fraudulently obtain welfare benefits or to vote and effectively legitimizes the criminal act of illegal immigration. The debate over licensing "shows the split over how to treat illegal immigrants," notes the *Chicago Tribune*. "Policymakers acknowledge their presence but remain torn over whether to treat them as criminals or as *de facto* members of society."

Despite government efforts to regulate immigration, the U.S. population includes millions of illegal immigrants who choose to ignore the law and become U.S. residents without official permission. Some sneak into the United States from Mexico or Canada without proper documentation. In 1996 alone the Border Patrol made 1.6 million apprehensions of people trying to enter the United States; most arrests occurred along the 1,952-mile U.S./ Mexico border. Other illegal immigrants receive permission to enter the United States on a temporary basis, as tourists or students for example, but then stay beyond the terms of their visas. These account for more than half of illegal immigrants in the United States. Still others may have lost their legal resident status after being convicted of a crime. Although Congress in 1986 attempted to "wipe the slate clean" by granting amnesty to most of America's illegal immigrant population at that time, the Immigration and Naturalization Service (INS) has estimated that five million illegal immigrants live in the United States. Other estimates, have gone as high as 11 million.

Critics of illegal immigration describe the presence of this number of illegal immigrants as an "invasion" that threatens the economic and social future of the United States. "The sovereignty of our nation is at risk from a flood of illegal immigrants who are usurping the benefits of being American citizens," writes columnist Ken Hamblin. Hamblin and others argue that the United States has limited resources and abilities to assimilate new immigrants and that greater efforts should be made to prevent people from entering illegally, deport illegal immigrants who are found here, and punish employers of illegal immigrants. "Cruel as it may seem," Hamblin argues, "we cannot afford compassion" because that would only encourage more illegal immigration.

However, efforts to deport or otherwise punish or deter illegal immigrants often strike people as too harsh and inhumane. Lisa Brodyaga, a lawyer for a refugee shelter in Harlingen, Texas, and immigrant rights advocate, has criticized recent federal statutes, including one requiring illegal immigrants to return to their country of origin and wait ten years before applying for a legal immigrant visa. "Do they [members of Congress] really believe that a person who has grown up here will leave the U.S. and wait 10 years to come back? Do they really believe that these new . . . laws will result in their stated goals [of] keeping people out who have been here illegally?" Brodyaga argues that these actions of Congress instead will create "an almost slave labor force—people who are undocumented, who are living here, and who can never claim their rights." Efforts should be made to include and treat illegal immigrants as full members of American society, Brodyaga and others argue, rather than try to exclude them or drive them away.

The question of whether to treat illegal immigrants as criminals, as victims, or as potential U.S. citizens lies at the heart of many of the debates about illegal immigration. The cartoons in the following chapter offer varying perspectives on America's illegal immigrants and its immigration policy.

# Examining Cartoon 1:
# "Surf's Up"

## About the Cartoon

Many people find the sheer number of illegal immigrants in the United States to be alarming. This cartoon depicts illegal immigrants as a literal tidal wave that threatens to swamp Uncle Sam, a symbol of the United States.

Estimates on the number of illegal immigrants in the United States range from 5 million (according to the Immigration and Naturalization Service) to more than 11 million (according to a Northeastern University study based on 2000 U.S. Census data). If the higher number is accurate, illegal immigrants constitute a little under 4 percent of America's total population.

## About the Cartoonist

Bill Garner is the editorial cartoonist for the *Washington Times*.

Garner. © 1986 by *Washington Times*. Reprinted with permission.

# Examining Cartoon 2:
## " ✭✿#! "

## About the Cartoon

In this cartoon of Uncle Sam on a scale, America's illegal immigrant population is compared to the unwanted pounds of a person trying to lose weight. Some observers argue that despite quotas that limit legal immigration, the United States readily accepts millions of additional (and illegal) immigrants by not strictly enforcing its immigration laws (especially rules against employing illegal immigrants). This is especially true during economic boom times when immigrants are desired for their labor. When America's economy goes sour, public sentiment against illegal immigration often grows, only to find out that illegal immigrants are harder to remove once they are established in this country. This cartoon was drawn in 1986, when the illegal immigrant population was estimated to be between 3 and 6 million and Congress was debating major immigration reforms.

## About the Cartoonist

J.D. Crowe began his career as a staff illustrator for the *Fort Worth Star-Telegram;* he shifted to political cartoons after one of his illustrations drew threats of a libel suit. He has since worked for the *San Diego Tribune* and the *Mobile Register.*

Crowe. © 1986 by *Fort Worth Star-Telegram.* Reprinted with permission of Copley Media Services.

# Examining Cartoon 3:
# "Illegals"

## About the Cartoon

More than half of the illegal immigrant population in the United States is from Mexico. In 1996 alone, the United States apprehended and returned 1.5 million Mexicans attempting to enter the country. Immigration critics have called for even more enforcement of American immigration laws, including increased deportations of illegal immigrants residing in the United States. A foreign perspective on America's efforts to return illegal immigrants can be seen in this cartoon. Uncle Sam, representing the United States, is set to catapult a group of Mexican "illegals" away. But among those being cast aside is the Statue of Liberty, which has for many years been celebrated as a symbol of America's welcoming embrace of poor immigrants from the world. The cartoon implies that the United States is casting aside this tradition of welcoming immigrants (and perhaps betraying its own fundamental values of freedom in the process).

## About the Cartoonist

Carlucho is the pen name of Carlos Villar Aleman, a Cuban-born cartoonist who now resides in Mexico. His work appears in both Mexican and U.S. publications, including *Newsweek* magazine.

Carlucho. © 1997 by Carlos Villar Aleman. Reprinted by permission of the Cartoonist and Writer's Syndicate.

# Examining Cartoon 4:
# "Give Me a Break"

## About the Cartoon

Unlike many other countries, the United States grants automatic citizenship to all people born within its borders, including children of illegal immigrants. Such "birthright citizenship" has its legal foundations in Supreme Court interpretations of the Fourteenth Amendment to the Constitution, which states that "all persons born or naturalized in the United States, and subject to the jurisdiction therof, are citizens of the United States." Critics have long argued that such a policy encourages and rewards illegal immigration and must be changed, by constitutional amendment if necessary. This opinion is reflected in this cartoon featuring the Statue of Liberty, a long-recognized symbol of America's welcoming attitude toward immigrants. At the statue's base is a poem by Emma Lazarus that includes the words "Give me your . . . huddled masses" (seen in the cartoon) that refer to refugees from other nations. The cartoon suggests that giving birthright citizenship to children of immigrants is taking America's tradition of generosity too far.

## About the Cartoonist

Michael Ramirez won the Pulitzer Prize for editorial cartooning in 1994 when he worked for the *Memphis Commercial Appeal*. He is now on the staff of the *Los Angeles Times;* his syndicated work also appears in *USA Today*.

Ramirez. © 1994 by Copley Media Services. Reprinted with permission.

# Examining Cartoon 5:
# "Maybe If We Refuse to Educate Their Kids . . ."

## About the Cartoon

A recurring debate over immigration has been over what public resources should be spent on illegal immigrants. One of the controversial elements of Proposition 187, a state initiative Californian
voters approved in 1994, was to bar illegal immigrants or their children from public schools. Advocates of the measure argued that
taxpayer money should not be spent on people who by law are not
supposed to be in the country. Critics of Proposition 187 argued that
children should not be punished for the actions of their parents and

that barring them from public schools would leave America with an uneducated underclass.

Although voters approved Proposition 187, implementation of its education provisions was stopped by federal judges who cited the 1982 case of *Plyler vs. Doe*, in which the U.S. Supreme Court ruled that all children, regardless of immigration status, have a constitutional right to a public education. Since then the debate over educating illegal immigrants and their children has continued within the U.S. Congress. This cartoon uses the conceit of American Indians responding to the first English settlers (the illegal immigrants of their time) to comment on this issue. It could be interpreted as expressing the argument that an education ban would not by itself prevent illegal immigrants from coming to America or make them leave once they got here, any more than American Indians could have prevented European settlers from arriving.

## About the Cartoonist

Jeff MacNelly served as the editorial cartoonist for the *Chicago Tribune* from 1982 until his death in 2000. His work received three Pulitzer Prizes and two National Cartoon Society Reuben Awards.

MacNelly. © 1996 by Tribune Media Services. Reprinted with permission.

# Examining Cartoon 6:
# "What Kinda Country Is This?"

## About the Cartoon

Each year hundreds of illegal immigrants perish when they attempt to enter the United States. Cubans trying to make it to the United States on homemade rafts or boats sometimes drown before completing the hundred-mile trip. Immigrants who attempt to bypass expanded border patrols on the U.S.-Mexican border find themselves stranded in deserts and sometimes perish from dehydration or exposure. Or, as referred to in this cartoon, some illegal immigrants who are smuggled into the United States in vans or trucks are tragically killed in crashes.

The topic in this cartoon is not so much illegal immigration itself, but what it says about American society. The newspaper reader on the left pronounces a litany of failings and problems of contemporary America and rhetorically asks "What kinda country is this, anyway?" The other newspaper reader, reading the headline "Immigrant Van Crashes," answers the question—the United States, despite its problems, remains a country that people will risk their lives to enter.

## About the Cartoonist

John Trever has been the cartoonist for the *Albuquerque Journal* since 1976. His work has been collected in *Trever's First Strike, The Trever Gallery: A Public Hanging (1992)*, and *The Trever Gallery Y2K*.

Trever. © 1999 by *Albuquerque Journal*. Reprinted by permission of King Features Syndicate.

# Chapter 3

# The Economic Effects of Illegal Immigration

# Preface

M ost experts agree that the primary motivation of many of America's illegal immigrants is the search for better jobs than those they can find in their countries of origin. For example, people who earn less than five hundred dollars yearly in China can make that or more in one week in America (often by working two or more jobs). The per capita income in Mexico is about one-tenth of that in the United States. To many immigrants, even a job paying less than three dollars per hour may seem attractive compared with their prospects at home.

Experts debate whether immigrants who come to America for such reasons harm or benefit the U.S. economy. Some economists argue that all Americans benefit from the labor of illegal immigrants. Consumers can enjoy lower prices for foods and goods because of low labor costs. Factories that might otherwise be moved offshore to take advantage of lower-cost labor remain in America because of immigrants. Furthermore, immigrants frequently take hard jobs that are often shunned by legal residents, such as outdoor landscaping, agricultural harvesting, and garment work.

However, some people claim that illegal immigrants cause economic harm to America, especially to poorer Americans who may compete with immigrants for jobs. Critics such as the Federation for American Immigration Reform (FAIR), a national lobbying group, argue that illegal immigrants, because of their tenuous legal status in the United States, are far less willing to complain to legal authorities, seek higher wages, or form unions. "Americans deserve decent jobs at decent wages," concludes FAIR, "not unfair competition from imported foreign workers who are exploited to the point of indentured servitude." The cartoons in this chapter offer differing perspectives on the economics of illegal immigration.

# Examining Cartoon 1:
# "What I Resent Is How They Steal Our Jobs"

## About the Cartoon

A common argument of illegal immigration's critics is that such immigrants take jobs that otherwise would go to Americans. This argument is voiced by a person in this cartoon but in a context that suggests that his views are probably not shared by the cartoonist. The complainer is pictured as a typical American lounging in his backyard. He and his wife are surrounded by gardeners, nannies, and maids—all occupations that are often performed by immigrants (both legal and illegal). The cartoon illustrates a common rebuttal to the immigrants-take-jobs assertion—illegal immigrants in fact take jobs (often unpleasant and low-paying jobs) that Americans are not inclined to do themselves. The cartoonist suggests that Americans often directly benefit from immigrant labor and have no cause to complain.

## About the Cartoonist

Mike Ritter is the editorial cartoonist for the Tribune Newspapers, a regional Arizona newspaper chain. His awards include three citations as best cartoonist by the Arizona Press Club.

Ritter. © 2001 by Mike Ritter. Reprinted by permission of King Features Syndicate.

# Examining Cartoon 2:
# "View from South of the Border"

## About the Cartoon

This 1996 cartoon by Ed Gamble comments on both U.S. enforcement of its immigration laws on the U.S.-Mexican border and on the economic motivators behind illegal immigration from America's southern neighbor. The United States officially prohibits unrestricted immigration from Mexico and has actually constructed fences on sections of its border to keep illegal immigrants out. However, many illegal immigrants from Mexico have successfully eluded enforcement and have found jobs, housing, and other social benefits in America. Would-be illegal immigrants receive a mixed message on whether America is serious about keeping them out, according to Gamble. This mixed message is also underscored by the sign's reference to the border being patrolled by "2 guards and 7 coyotes." A "coyote" is a term for a professional smuggler who for a fee helps illegal immigrants enter the country.

## About the Cartoonist

Ed Gamble joined the *Florida Times-Union* in Jacksonville as its first staff political cartoonist in 1980. His honors include two Florida Press Association awards.

Gamble. © 1996 by Ed Gamble. Reprinted with permission.

# Examining Cartoon 3:
# "Two Choices"

## About the Cartoon

Many people on both sides of the immigration debate agree that a desire to improve one's economic status motivates much illegal immigration. Chuck Asay follows this assumption in this cartoon and presents two possible responses. In the first frame, a person in a Border Patrol uniform urges that a wall be built between the United States and the "country next door" (presumably Mexico) to prevent illegal immigrants from entering. In the second frame, a businessperson representing "trade" argues that instead of a wall, a factory should be built in the "country next door." The cartoon was drawn in 1994, the year that the controversial North American Free Trade Agreement (NAFTA) went into effect. Under NAFTA, the governments of the United States, Canada, and Mexico, agreed to lower tariffs and trade barriers among themselves. Supporters of NAFTA argued that it would spur investment and job growth in Mexico and thus reduce illegal immigration from that country.

## About the Cartoonist

Chuck Asay, a two-time winner of the H.L. Mencken Award, decided he wanted to be a cartoonist when he was in the eighth grade. He is the editorial cartoonist for the *Colorado Springs Gazette Telegraph;* his work is also nationally syndicated.

Asay. © 1994 by *Colorado Springs Gazette Telegraph.* Reprinted by permission of Creators Syndicate, Inc.

# Chapter 4

# Illegal Immigration and National Security Concerns

# Preface

Prior to September 11, 2001, much of the debate over illegal immigration in the United States focused on economic and cultural issues. The terrorist attacks of September 11, in which hijacked jetliners crashed into buildings and killed thousands, propelled national security to the forefront of illegal immigration concerns. Public anxieties were raised especially by the revelation that the attacks were carried out by foreign-born terrorists, some of whom had overstayed their business or tourist visas and were residing in the United States illegally.

The Immigration and Naturalization Service (INS) came under heavy criticism following the terrorist attacks, especially when one of its offices mistakenly sent paperwork reauthorizing student visas to two of the September 11 terrorists months after the incident. Critics argued that the INS should do a far better job of keeping track of America's immigrant population, especially those who enter on temporary visas and then remain illegally in the country. In the year following September 11, 2001, the federal government detained twelve hundred foreigners on terrorist suspicions; most were never charged but were later deported for immigration violations. The INS began a program to require fingerprinting and registration of foreign visitors from selected countries. Additional legislation passed in 2002 requires the government to put into place by 2005 an automated exit-entry tracking system for all foreign visitors. Some immigrant advocate and civil liberties groups have condemned these actions for being both wasteful law enforcement diversions and affronts to the civil rights of immigrants. The cartoons in this chapter examine various facets of the debate over the relationship between immigration and national security.

# Examining Cartoon 1:
# "I Don't Think They're Too Smart . . ."

"I DON'T THINK THEY'RE TOO SMART... THEY SPELLED 'TOURIST'... 'T·E·R·R·O·R·I·S·T' ON THEIR VISA..."

## About the Cartoon

Many of America's illegal residents do not enter the country illegally but instead obtain temporary student or tourist visas. Once in the country, they then violate the terms of their visas either by staying longer than authorized or by not following through on their stated intention. A 2002 report of the Center for Immigration Studies examined forty-eight individuals linked with terrorist activity (including the September 11, 2001, attacks) and found that sixteen of them entered the United States on tourist or other temporary visas.

This 1999 cartoon depicts people who are obviously Middle Eastern terrorists (to the point of stereotype), but who are nonetheless allowed to enter the country by oblivious immigration officials. The cartoon and its caption make an exaggerated point of how foreign terrorists are exploiting loopholes (and stupidity) in America's system of immigration control.

## About the Cartoonist

Bill Schorr is the staff editorial cartoonist for the *New York Daily News*. He has previously worked for the *Kansas City Star* and the *Los Angeles Herald Examiner.*

Schorr. © 1997 by *New York Daily News*. Reprinted by permission of United Features Syndicate.

# Examining Cartoon 2:
# "News Item . . ."

## About the Cartoon

Both before and after the terrorist attacks of September 11, 2001, various experts and government panels suggested ways of keeping greater track of America's immigrants. One recurring proposal has been to establish a central computerized data bank and national identification card system to keep track of America's citizens, temporary visitors, and immigrants. In this 1994 cartoon, cartoonist Chuck Asay imagines such a system in action. A woman buying groceries finds that not only are her groceries being electronically scanned (for pricing), but that she herself is then scanned to see if she "checks out" as a legal U.S. citizen or resident. Asay probably does not believe in the literal sense that Americans would actually have barcodes tattooed on their foreheads and be checked by fearsome-looking federal agents. But his cartoon is an expression of his fear of a federal government that has too much power to collect information and pry into the affairs of individuals—somewhat like the "big brother" totalitarian government described in George Orwell's novel *1984.*

## About the Cartoonist

Chuck Asay, a two-time winner of the H.L. Mencken Award, decided he wanted to be a cartoonist when he was in the eighth grade. He is the editorial cartoonist for the *Colorado Springs Gazette Telegraph;* his work is also nationally syndicated.

Asay. © 1994 by *Colorado Springs Gazette Telegraph.* Reprinted by permission of Creators Syndicate, Inc.

# Examining Cartoon 3:
# "Department of Student Visas"

## About the Cartoon

On March 11, 2002, exactly six months after the September 11, 2001, terrorist attacks, officials at a flight school in Florida received official notification from the Immigration and Naturalization Service (INS) that student visas for Mohamed Atta and Marwan Al-Shehhi had been approved. Both individuals, who had entered the United States on temporary tourist visas, had already gone through flight training at the school; both had participated in the suicidal terrorist missions of September 11 in which planes were crashed into the World Trade Center and the Pentagon.

The revelations unleashed a storm of criticism against the INS. Critics argued that the mailing was emblematic of how slow and incompetent the INS bureaucracy had become; some called for the agency's abolishment. This cartoon, published shortly after this particular scandal, expresses this argument by having silent movie stars Stan Laurel and Oliver Hardy portray a pair of INS workers approving student visa applications. Laurel and Hardy were popular film stars of the 1920s and 1930s who always played a pair of bumbling incompetents.

## About the Cartoonist

Since 1979, Gary Brookins has been the editorial cartoonist for the *Richmond Times-Dispatch*. His work has won multiple awards from the Virginia Press Association.

Brookins. © 2002 by *Richmond Times-Dispatch*. Reprinted by permission of King Features Syndicate.

# Organizations to Contact

The editors have compiled the following list of organizations concerned with the issues debated in this book. The descriptions are derived from materials provided by the organizations. All have publications or information available for interested readers. This list was compiled on the date of publication of the present volume; the information provided here may change. Be aware that many organizations take several weeks or longer to respond to inquiries, so allow as much time as possible.

**American Friends Service Committee (AFSC)**
1501 Cherry St., Philadelphia, PA 19102
(215) 241-7000 • fax: (215) 241-7275
e-mail: afscinfo@afsc.org • website: www.afsc.org

The AFSC is a Quaker organization that attempts to relieve human suffering and find new approaches to world peace and social justice through nonviolence. It lobbies against what it believes to be unfair immigration laws, especially sanctions criminalizing the employment of illegal immigrants. It has published *Sealing Our Borders: The Human Toll*, a report documenting human rights violations committed by law enforcement agents against immigrants.

**Center for Immigration Studies (CIS)**
1522 K St. NW, Suite 820, Washington, DC 20005-1202
(202) 466-8185 • fax: (202) 466-8076
e-mail: center@cisorg • website: www.cis.org

CIS studies the effects of immigration on the economic, social, demographic, and environmental conditions in the United States. It believes that the large number of recent immigrants has become a burden on America and favors reforming immigration laws to make them consistent with U.S. interests. The center publishes reports, position papers, and the quarterly journal *Scope*.

**Federation for American Immigration Reform (FAIR)**
1666 Connecticut Ave. NW, Suite 400, Washington, DC 20009
(202) 328-7004 • fax: (202) 387-3447
e-mail: info@fairus.org • website: www.fairus.org

FAIR works to stop illegal immigration and to limit legal immigration. It believes that the growing flood of immigrants into the United States causes higher unemployment and taxes social services. FAIR has published many reports and position papers, including *Ten Steps to Securing America's Borders* and *Immigration 2000: The Century of the New American Sweatshop*.

**The National Network for Immigrant and Refugee Rights**
310 Eighth St., Suite 307, Oakland, CA 94607
(510) 465-1984 • fax: (510) 465-1885
website: www.nnirr.org

The network includes community, church, labor, and legal groups committed to the cause of equal rights for all immigrants. These groups work to end discrimination and unfair treatment of illegal immigrants and refugees. The network aims to strengthen and coordinate educational efforts among immigration advocates nationwide. It publishes a monthly newsletter, *Network News*.

**United States Immigration and Naturalization Service (INS)**
425 I St. NW, Room 4236, Washington, DC 20536
(202) 514-4316
website: www.ins.usdoj.gov

The INS is charged with enforcing immigration laws and regulations, as well as administering immigrant-related services including the granting of asylum and refugee status. It produces numerous reports and evaluations on selected programs. Statistics and information on immigration and immigration  laws as well as congressional testimony, fact sheets, and other materials are available on its website.

# For Further Research

## Books

Brent Ashabranner, *Our Beckoning Borders: Illegal Immigration to America*. New York: Cobblehill Books, 1996.

Roy Beck, *The Case Against Immigration*. New York: W.W. Norton, 1996.

Peter Brimelow, *Alien Nation: Common Sense About America's Immigration Disaster*. New York: Random House, 1995.

Leo R. Chavez, *Shadowed Lives: Undocumented Immigrants in American Society*. Fort Worth, TX: Harcourt Brace College Publishers, 1997.

Roger Daniels and Otis L. Graham, *Debating American Immigration, 1882–Present*. Lanham, MD: Roman & Littlefield, 2001.

David W. Haines and Karen Elaine Rosenblum, eds., *Illegal Immigration in America: A Reference Handbook*. Westport, CT: Greenwood Press, 1999.

William Hawkins, *Importing Revolution: Open Borders and the Radical Agenda*. Monterey, VA: American Immigration Control Foundation, 1995.

Helene Hayes, *U.S. Immigration Policy and the Undocumented: Ambivalent Laws, Furtive Lies*. Westport, CT: Praeger, 2001.

Peter Kwong, *Forbidden Workers: Illegal Chinese Immigrants and American Labor*. New York: New Press, 1998.

Juan F. Perea, ed., *Immigrants Out! The New Nativism and the Anti-Immigrant Impulse in the United States*. New York: New York University Press, 1997.

Mei Ling Rein et al., eds., *Immigration and Illegal Aliens: Burden or Blessing?* Wylie, TX: Information Plus, 1999.

Sebastian Rotella, *Twilight on the Line: Underworlds and Politics at the U.S.-Mexico Border.* New York: W.W. Norton, 1998.

**Periodicals**

T. Alexander Aleinikoff, "Illegal Employers," *American Prospect,* December 4, 2000.

George M. Anderson, "Punishing the Immigrant," *America,* February 19, 2001.

David Bacon, "Labor and Immigrant Workers," *Z Magazine,* October 2000.

Roy Beck, "Rewarding Illegal Aliens," *Social Contract,* Spring 1999.

*Business Week,* "Keep America's Gates Open. Just Watch Them Better," November 19, 2001.

Layne Cameron, "The Frontlines of Illegal Immigration," *American Legion,* March 2001.

Wade Graham, "Masters of the Game: How the U.S. Protects the Traffic in Cheap Mexican Labor," *Harper's Magazine,* July 1996.

William P. Hoar, "Rewarding Illegal Aliens," *New American,* August 26, 2002.

Donald Kerwin, "Crossing the Border: The U.S.-Mexico Borderland Has Seen Thousands of Deaths," *America,* December 9, 2002.

Mark Krikorian, "Illegal Means a Lot," *National Review,* June 16, 1997.

Carol Nagengast, "Militarizing the Border Patrol," *NACLA Report on the Americas,* November/December 1998.

Kate O'Beirne, "The Bush INS: Time for Accountability," *National Review,* December 9, 2002.

Robert Park, "One Man's Border Battle: An Interview with Roger Barnett," *Social Contract,* Fall 2000.

Margot Roosevelt et al., "Illegal but Fighting for Rights," *Time,* January 22, 2001.

Daniel W. Sutherland, "Revinventing the Border," *Reason,* April 1999.

# Index